NATURE DETECTIVES

A walk in the park

Jo Waters

Heinemann
LIBRARY

Little Nippers

www.heinemann.co.uk/library
Visit our website to find out more information about **Heinemann Library** books.

To order:
☎ Phone 44 (0) 1865 888066
📠 Send a fax to 44 (0) 1865 314091
💻 Visit the Heinemann Bookshop at www.heinemann.co.uk/library to browse our catalogue and order online.

First published in Great Britain by Heinemann Library, Halley Court, Jordan Hill, Oxford OX2 8EJ, part of Harcourt Education. Heinemann is a registered trademark of Harcourt Education Ltd.

Editorial: Kathy Peltan and Clare Lewis
Design: Jo Hinton-Malivoire and
   Tinstar Design Ltd (www.tinstar.co.uk)
Picture Research: Maria Joannou and Rebecca Sodergren
Production: Camilla Smith

Originated by Dot Gradations Ltd.
Printed and bound in China by South China Printing Company

13-digit ISBN 978 0 431 17161 6 (hardback)
10 09 08 07 06
10 9 8 7 6 5 4 3 2 1

13-digit ISBN 978 0 431 17166 1 (paperback)
11 10 09 08 07
10 9 8 7 6 5 4 3 2 1

British Library Cataloguing in Publication Data
Waters, Jo
578.7'55
Nature Detectives – A Walk in the Park
A full catalogue record for this book is available from the British Library.

Acknowledgements
The Publishers would like to thank the following for permission to reproduce photographs:
Alamy Images p. 5; Alamy Images/Anthony Collins p. 20; Corbis pp. 15, 21; Corbis/Jacqui Hurst p.11; Corbis/Ralph A Clevenger p. 8; Corbis/Phil Schermeister p. 16; FLPA p. 9; FLPA/Jurgen & Christine Sohns p. 13; Harcourt Education Ltd/Malcolm Harris pp. 4, 6, 14, 17, 23; Getty Images/Botanica p.7; Getty Images /Photographers Choice p. 10; Masterfile/Matt Brasier p. 22; Photolibrary.com/Oxford Scientific Films pp. 12, 18, 19.

Cover photograph reproduced with permission of Getty Images.

Our thanks to Annie Davy and Michael Scott for their assistance in the preparation of this book.

Every effort has been made to contact copyright holders of any material reproduced in this book. Any omissions will be rectified in subsequent printings if notice is given to the Publishers.

Contents

Into the park

Where are we?
We are at the park!

Lots of people have fun here.

Fabulous flowers

Look at the flowers.
Can you see the petals?

petals

Busy bees buzz around
the flowers.

Another visitor

Who else is visiting the flowers?

A colourful butterfly!

9

Grass

Each *blade* of grass is a leaf.

Down in the grass
little snails are hiding.

11

Spotty minibeast

Who is climbing up the stalk?
A ladybird!

12

Ladybirds have lots of spots.
How many can you see?

Wiggly worm

Worms live in the earth.
They wiggle in the mud!

Who is hiding?

Sitting in the tree ...
a squirrel!

What could he be eating?

19

On the pond

A duck and her babies go for a swim. Quack quack!

20

Look closer. A duck's feather is made of lots of tiny hairs.

Goodbye park

The sun is going down.
It's getting chilly. Brrr.

Smell one last flower.
It's time to go home.

23

Index

Notes for adults

This series encourages children to explore their environment to gain knowledge and understanding of the things they can see, smell, hear, taste, and feel. The following Early Learning Goals are relevant to the series:

• use the senses to explore and learn about the world around them
• investigate objects and materials by using all of their senses as appropriate
• find out about living things, objects and events they observe
• observe and identify features in the place they live and the natural world
• find out about their environment, and talk about those features they like and dislike.

The following additional information may be of interest

Exploring the natural world at an early age can help promote awareness of the environment and general understanding of life processes. Discussing the seasons with children can be a good way of helping them understand the concepts of time, patterns and change. Identifying features that people share with insects and animals can promote understanding of similarities.

Follow-up activities

• Encourage children to think and talk about why people should take care of the environment and not damage plants or harm animals.
• Encourage children to use all their senses to feel, look at, and describe a leaf. Invite comments about all aspects of leaves, including colour, texture, smell and sound.
• The children could make a collage or leaf prints as part of an art session.

24